THE JOB INNERVIEW

A Guide to How to Mindfully Prepare For Your Job Interview

Y. PAL

*This book is dedicated to all those striving for greatness
and working towards a better tomorrow.*

Table of Contents

Preface

Job interviewing is one of the most important but easily overlooked parts of your career. It determines your professional pathway and can make the difference between successfully landing your dream job or having to settle for a second-rate option. Settling for your current role or a situation where your development is stagnating, or taking a role in which you aren't really invested, negatively impacts you and your career.

Let's be honest: Interviewing can be an uncomfortable experience. Putting yourself out there, as a new job seeker or even as a seasoned career professional, goes against key fundamental principles of human nature related to self-preservation. You are wired to avoid exposing yourself to rejection, and the interview process puts you in danger of being told "thanks, but no thanks." However, your interview experience does not have to turn out this way – if you prepare effectively.

Regardless of where you are in your career, meaningful interview preparation can take a lot of time and effort. This is all relative to how much you want to; set off in the right direction with your first position, further your career with your next job or announce yourself professionally by stepping into your dream role. Your previous approach to interview preparation probably didn't work as well as it could have, preventing you from standing out against the competition.

By investing in this book, you've taken the first step towards recognizing that interviewing requires more than simply researching a company, applying for an open position, and thinking about a few questions to ask if you're chosen for an interview. You need a more holistic approach to your preparation in order to drive your personal success and to purposefully present yourself as a leader. This book will provide you with a blueprint of how to fully prepare yourself, internally and externally, for the interview process. Together, we will cover areas of personal consideration and reflection, as well as provide you with information, knowledge, and best practices in job interviews, enabling you to plan more effectively. Chapter summaries will provide an overview of key takeaways to assist you. Your journey towards positively showing recruiters and hiring managers what you see in yourself starts now.

Your career journey

How you interview will affect your overall career path. Will you move into a role that you have identified as optimal for honing your skills and furthering your development? Will you be able to fast-track your career path in line with your expectations? Or will you need to settle for a non-preferred option? The significance of how you prepare to interview matters a lot.

Introduction

Before you begin your journey as a job seeker, you need to come to terms with the fact that the odds are against you. This isn't meant to discourage you, but the reality is that for every open position, there are hundreds of applicants, and only one successful candidate will be hired. Only your best efforts in terms of applying yourself in your preparation will enable you to land the role you truly deserve. Every job interview you prepare for is a learning experience. Interviewing well is an art and a skill. Each interview is an opportunity to build your personal comfort with this process.

Preparing to interview effectively involves both internal and external preparation. Think of preparation overall as an iceberg: your internal preparation lies below the water and represents your motivations, mental readiness, and mindfulness. These elements, which are personal and affect your interior self, enable you to align your conscious thoughts and actions with your behaviors, setting you up for success as you interview.

The part showing above the water represents your external preparation; this is what is visible and subsequently measured through your connections with the interview process, i.e. your interactions with recruitment team members, hiring managers and organizational stakeholders. External preparation focuses on how you interact with each person during an interview process, from the moment when your resume reaches a recruiter, to screening interviews over the phone, to final in-person interviews. Your preparation here will impact how you conduct yourself in conversations, how you respond to specific questions during your interview(s), and how you present yourself as a viable and strong candidate overall. Understanding the elements of internal and external preparation and applying yourself to each area is key to the interview process. The overall goal of this book is to empower you to remain true to yourself while enabling you to outshine everyone else as you seek to take that next step in your career.

Preparing to interview effectively

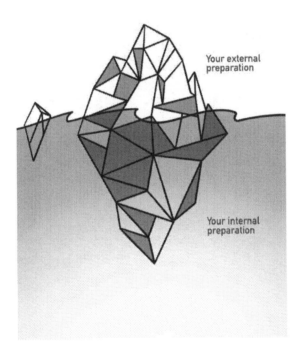

Both external and internal aspects make up effective interview preparation. Be prepared to invest your time in both for the best results.

For the most comprehensive guide to interview preparation, we recommend that you read this book through in order, reflecting on each of the key learnings at the end of each chapter. Understanding your inner self and internal preparation are covered in section 1, with the focus shifting to external preparation, enabling you to create a strong initial connection in section 2. Finally, section 3 focuses on key preparation aspects related to your interview(s), the culmination of your journey. While each section builds upon the previous ones, you can of course skip ahead to a particular chapter if you are looking for specific guidance related to where you are in your overall interview preparation.

Section 1: Internal preparation

Understanding your story and background

Section Introduction

The practice of preparing for an interview involves a variety of pre-interview actions and reflections. Ideally this should occur prior to your decision to assess the job market for opportunities. Multiple factors need to be internalized and recognized as part of your overall preparation process in order to interview effectively.

The following two chapters dive into these pre-interview preparation techniques, introducing and reviewing essential aspects of individual motivation and mentality which will directly impact your ability to engage with interviewers at the levels necessary to present yourself as a top candidate for an open position.

Chapter 1: Targeted motivation

Understanding your values, career, and background

This chapter highlights the importance of understanding who you are and the power that you have as a job seeker. An essential concept to your overall preparation is that "your decisions shape your destiny." To build this into a framework related to your job search, it is worth noting that you own the decision as it relates to what you focus on, by determining which jobs you will apply for. This personal selection process manifests itself in the form of your individual drive and motivation to prepare for your interview and to truly push yourself to succeed.

The truth is that preparing for an interview starts long before a recruiter picks up the phone or sends an email requesting a follow up conversation or screening interview. To enable yourself to be fully motivated and to prepare for a successful interview(s), it's important to be self-aware and mindful when you start applying for jobs. Ask yourself the following questions as you reflect on your upcoming journey:

1. Where am I in my career and what am I trying to achieve?

Whether you are just starting out in your career or are an experienced professional with years of experience, it's important to understand your aims and goals as they relate to your job search.

For example, a recent college graduate might prioritize job opportunities which provide them with technical training and developmental coaching, while an experienced professional might be looking for roles that would enable them to advance to project management or managing teams and individuals.

Being aware of your goals gives you more motivation when you are given the opportunity to interview for a role with characteristics that align with them. Moreover, it also grounds you in how you plan to present yourself to recruiters and hiring managers, most of whom will question your intent and motivations for joining their organization. Apply this self-awareness when you review open roles, and you will set yourself up for success.

2. What are my internal wants and needs as they relate to my job search?

A key component of motivation is being mindful of your wants and needs and how a prospective role meet those needs. Simply put, you will prepare to succeed in your job interview(s) and push yourself harder if the return, from your perspective, is worthwhile. Increased monetary compensation is a key driver for many individuals of course. However, you need to look deeper than that. Nowadays, greater employee benefits are a significant factor to consider, as well as work flexibility, and these may be more valuable to you in the long run than a simple increase in take-home pay. You may realize that your earning potential is capped at your current employer, or that you are missing out on various industry benefits that other employees with your experience level are receiving. It's important to understand these internal factors, as they will further motivate you during the interview planning and preparation phases and the subsequent interview process.

3. What organizations do I personally identify with?

Ask yourself this simple question: if this organization were to call me with good news about my application, how excited would I be at the opportunity? If your reaction is anything less than 10 out of 10, you may want to re-consider your application. If you don't really want the job, you will not be fully motivated to prepare appropriately, and your career will be better off in the long term if you focus your efforts on finding something that is better aligned with your interests and aspirations.

Understanding your motivations is key to preparing effectively.

Reflective exercises

These questions are intended to really make you think about your core feelings, your values, and what really will bring meaning into your job seeking and preparation. Tools that can assist in this space include putting together a vision or values board to assist with your self-reflection and researching organizations on websites such as Glassdoor and LinkedIn to further understand employee offerings and corporate values, as you look for organizations whose offerings align with your priorities.

Example of what a vision and values board tied to a job search could look like.

Glassdoor and LinkedIn are valuable tools in gaining insight into prospective organizations you are considering.

Chapter Summary

Working through each of these three questions safeguards you from misaligning yourself with roles that don't tie in with your personal values and what you are striving for. Answering them for yourself ensures that, once contacted for a position, you are fully engaged and motivated to prepare for the interview process, and are ready to put your best foot forward.

The job market is highly competitive, and the biggest mistake you can make is not being inspired by the opportunity at hand, which is a product of misaligning yourself with roles at organizations that you are not fully committed to or really interested in. You have to realize that this misalignment wastes your valuable time – time that you could be spending in further developing your skills, expertise, and experience, aspects that will enable you to outshine the competition when your next real interview opportunity comes knocking.

Key takeaway: it's essential to acknowledge that preparing for an interview begins with self-awareness and self-reflection at the very beginning, when you are initially deciding to enter the job market.

Being self-aware of your motivations gives you the clarity to apply yourself fully.

Chapter 2: Building a strong mentality

In the previous chapter, we discussed the concept of targeted motivation and being self-aware, enabling you to set yourself up for more empowered preparation and truly applying yourself. Your mentality throughout this process is the second factor which, coupled with your motivation and external preparation, will set you apart from other candidates. Successfully landing your dream job will require a strong mentality to properly harness and channel your motivation. This chapter seeks to provide you with the self-reflective tools and insights necessary to sharpen your mental approach to job hunting, a key aspect of the overall interview preparation matrix.

Think of your motivation as the fire that keeps you working towards your goals, hopes and dreams, and your mentality as the furnace which houses and contains this fire.

There are six key areas of focus that relate to building a strong mentality. These include embracing uncertainty, leveraging anxiety, building attentiveness and focus, embracing togetherness and reducing interference, harnessing the power of visualization, and grounding oneself in thankfulness. In this chapter, we will explore each in detail. Each area may resonate with you differently; you may feel more of a connection to some than to others. While this may be the case, understand that they're all important – each has a role in furthering your mentality. In our exploration of these areas, we'll provide examples of how you can practically further your relationship with each.

Building a strong mentality – uncertainty

The Academy of Management Journal[1] reported that job searching is one of the most grueling tasks you'll ever undertake, because it is highly autonomous, self-organized, loosely structured and ill-defined, with feedback rare. The overall process of interviewing is highly uncertain; it is the value of uncertainty that you will face which must be recognized and internally reconciled. The uncertainty to come, if viewed as an opportunity and not something uncomfortable to be endured, will enable you to prepare and perform at your natural best, easily outshining other candidates. Further, truly acknowledging and valuing uncertainty will enable you to ground yourself appropriately in your environment (the job-seeking process), resulting in a heightened ability to maintain positivity, focus, and application.

There are various ways to build these "uncertainty muscles" within your mentality. One such method is to practice exploration in your personal life. Try something new that you have been putting off, like a bucket list item or an unusual activity. Feeling what it is like to focus in an unfamiliar situation will enable you to build and strengthen the mental aspects which enable you to embrace uncertainty with vigor and eagerness, as opposed to nervousness and anxiety. The world of uncertainty, when positively

---

[1] Adams, S (2012) Job Search Depressing You? Try A Little Harder, https://www.forbes.com/sites/susanadams/2012/04/30/losing-your-job-how-it-affects-your-mental-health/?sh=4017b4d6567b

appreciated, forms a key pillar in building a strong mentality and effectively preparing for the interview process.

Building a strong mentality – Addressing anxiety

Feeling anxious or nervous at the thought of interviewing is natural. Statistics reflect that 73% of job seekers feel that looking for a new job is one of the most stressful things in life[2]. To effectively overcome your anxiety, you must mentally embrace these feelings and channel them into positive actions. These actions are directly associated with your ability to present yourself in a way that will enable you to highlight your work ethic and strengths against other candidates (discussed further in later chapters).

Practices that will enable you to positively harness your anxiety involve reflection and review. Approach anxiety by performing a self-analysis of issues that are bothering you and why; create a list and put in some time researching each of them. If your research supports their significance, make a plan for how to address them. Mentally making peace with your anxiety factors and harnessing them for positive energy can be as simple as talking to others who have undertaken a similar decision-making process, or else are a part of the environment you wish to join. You could, for example, attend local networking events to learn more about the corporate culture of a potential employer you wish to interview for, or reach out to a recruiter to understand what's expected of new hires before you apply. If your self-analysis leads you to doubting your technical proficiency for a specific skillset the job requires, you can assess your abilities to know exactly where you stand and address any gaps through self-study or e-learning modules to build your confidence.

---

[2] Skillings, P (2021) Face the Fear: How to Overcome Job Interview Anxiety, https://biginterview.com/interview-anxiety/

Networking allows you the opportunity to make connections, gain insight into an organization or department, and ask questions.

Effectively understanding and embracing your anxiety, by channeling such emotions into positive actions, will enable you to offset negative thoughts, furthering your overall interview preparation by empowering you with the knowledge required to address your challenges and be confident within yourself.

Building a strong mentality – attentiveness & focus

The journey towards obtaining a truly fulfilling job is often described as a marathon and not a sprint. This analogy refers not only to the time you'll spend as a prospective job seeker – which can be lengthy indeed – but also the difficulties associated with preparing for and undergoing the interviews required. Indeed, preparing for an interview necessitates high levels of attentiveness and focus, requiring a mentality that embraces both.

It is important to understand that while you are preparing to interview, life will continue; there will be various distractions that will demand your attention. Recognize that a strong mentality will guide you here, allowing you to spend no more time on these areas than necessary. As the philosopher Marcus Aurelius[3] once wrote, "The value of attentiveness varies in proportion to its object." An individual's ability to disregard unrelated things is just as important as their ability to focus on what's required, a practice which is highly relevant to you as you prepare yourself for upcoming interviews.

Investing in yourself is the best method to help you build your attentiveness and focus. Commitment to practices like journaling, meditation, and exercise support your ability to concentrate, filter out distractions, and effectively manage your emotions[4]. Try going for a morning jog; hit the gym or meditate before your day starts. These "attentiveness training" practices enable you to build your inner strength, which can be utilized to focus on what matters. This forms a key element of your overall interview preparation.

Building a strong mentality – togetherness & reducing interference

It is important to understand that while your ability to prepare for and interview effectively is a highly individual pursuit, the concept of togetherness is valuable both for building a strong mentality and ensuring your mental health. This can include your significant other, roommates, friends and family – whoever you spend time with and depend upon. Your support network is vitally important during your interview preparation. In particular, they'll play an important role by limiting distractions and reducing interference in your life, thus enhancing your attentiveness and focus and positively influencing your interview preparation. Further, togetherness also forms a key pillar of your mental health, by providing an

---

[3] Feloni, R (2016) 9 timeless lessons from the great Roman emperor Marcus Aurelius, https://www.businessinsider.com/lessons-from-marcus-aurelius-2016-2#dont-spend-time-worrying-about-frivolous-people-who-have-no-positive-impact-on-others-1

[4] Oppong, T (2019) The distracted mind (How to increase your attention span) https://medium.com/personal-growth/the-distracted-mind-how-to-increase-your-attention-span-15765212fae7

outlet or sounding board for your self-analysis and discovery as you progress through the different stages of interview preparation for prospective jobs.

Practice togetherness by connecting directly with those near and dear to you. Explain your job search and focus areas, and highlight how they can support you during this important time. This can be as simple as spreading household duties around or understanding that you may require more time to yourself than usual, to facilitate your preparation for interviewing. It is important to talk with your loved ones about your job search. Approaching them in an open manner further promotes commitment from you personally to follow through on your goals.

While certain aspects of your lifestyle may need to be sacrificed in the short term, ensuring you are present in the moment on a daily basis will enable your support network to avoid feeling isolated and underappreciated. It is crucial to appreciate the value of your support network and to actively embrace everyone who's a part of it. Just as it takes a village to raise a child, your interview success is also partly a product of those who support you during this period. Do not forget this.

Embracing togetherness is an important component of your overall mental health and internal preparation.

Building a strong mentality - Visualization

In the past you may have visualized living through your worst-case interview questions or horror interview scenarios. This may seem like the best way to prepare for adversity, but it's counterproductive. Fight the urge to do this and focus on positive visualizations to prepare more effectively and to center your mentality. Indeed, a lot has been written about the immense power of visualization, with professional athletes such as Serena Williams and sports teams such as the San Francisco 49ers incorporating mental imagery sessions into their training programs. You don't have to be a professional athlete to benefit from the power of visualization, though. As you prepare your mind for the interview process, visualizing or mentally picturing your future achievements can positively translate to heightened performance and better outcomes.

It is noteworthy to recognize that we stimulate the same portion of the brain when we visualize an action as when we are actually performing this action. Consequently, through visualizing outcomes and positive imagery, it's possible to prepare your brain for a successful interview. To help you reflect and apply visualization as part of your preparation, consider embracing the following process on a daily basis:

1. Find a quiet, comfortable space that you can use. The best time to practice visualization is when you are completely relaxed; in the evening before bed or first thing in the morning are good times.
2. Close your eyes and calmly breathe in and out. Repeat this three times. Feel free to experiment with lying down or sitting upright.
3. Break down your goal and visualize yourself undertaking each step towards its achievement. You may choose to visualize yourself preparing purposefully for your interview; updating your resume and online profile, dedicating time daily to the practice of finding open roles which excite you, building networking connections and increasing your technical expertise. Picture yourself in each of these moments; imagine what you are positively experiencing and feeling. This process will leave you invigorated and looking forward to your interview preparation.
4. Visualize your future self successfully dealing with challenges associated with interviewing. Imagine the experience from your own point of view; for example, you could visualize yourself answering interview questions easily without any signs of nerves or anxiety. Eventually, when you are actually asked to interview, you can prepare by utilizing the power of visualization to picture the interview. Imagine you are entering the building – your future office – and being greeted by your interviewer, your future boss, making a great impression and leaving the interview room with a job offer imminent. This is known as mental rehearsal, and enables you to create a positive experience in your mind which in turn will influence your physical performance of the same experience when you approach it.
5. Use the power of affirmations to further strengthen your visualizations. Write a statement down that describes the

outcome you are seeking. For example, "I will make the most of every networking opportunity to find out more about this organization," "I will outwork all other candidates in my preparation." Post this statement in a visible area, such as by your desk, or wherever you spend time preparing for your upcoming interviews. These affirmations will keep you grounded and act as a further tool to assist you in visualizing your desired outcome while you are working towards it.

Harnessing the power of visualization is vital in building a strong mentality, a key aspect of your preparation for a successful interview. To do so effectively, you need to picture things happening which align to your goals on a daily basis, using illustrative moments and mental imagery. By truly envisioning yourself carrying out these actions and really believing in them, they are more likely to transpire in real life, thanks to your having already lived through them mentally.

Trust in the power of visualization as a way to prepare yourself for a successful interview.

Building a strong mentality - Thankfulness

To further build a strong mentality as part of your interview preparation, embrace a state of thankfulness. Individuals who foster such a mindset heighten their feelings of positivity and appreciation for all they have. Related to your interview preparation, this enables you to bolster your self-confidence and worldview, by directly helping you achieve greater levels of growth, happiness, positivity, and joy, while experiencing less stress and negativity[56].

When you focus on thankfulness and appreciating what you have, your mind shifts from acknowledging what you don't have to recognizing the great opportunities available to you. For example, instead of focusing on the anxiety associated with interviewing for a job, an individual with a thankfulness mindset will see amazing opportunities to further individual

5 Pettit, M (2020) 6 Ways to Start Developing a Gratitude Mindse,
https://thriveglobal.com/stories/6-ways-to-start-developing-a-gratitude-mindset/

6 Forsythe, M (2020) How to Calm Your Nerves Before A Job Interview,
https://www.berkley-group.com/how-to-calm-your-nerves-before-a-job-interview/

growth, and a host of learning experiences that they'll be exposed to through the process.

Embracing thankfulness will further your appreciation of the interview journey and the numerous opportunities at hand.

Approaches to harness as you strengthen your state of thankfulness include:

1. Treating everything as a learning experience – you will better prepare to interview overall if you go into the process with an open mind.

2. Acknowledging what works – find joy in the process and what is going well, whether it's learning more about your dream organization through your research or speaking to a recruiter to understand the duties of open positions; be thankful for the progress you make on a daily basis.

3. Looking to give back to your community – research has shown that, by assisting in raising the spirts of others, individuals are able to gain as much positivity as the person being helped with both increasing their level of thankfulness significantly.

4. Staying mindfully grateful –People with heightened levels of thankfulness and gratitude are generally more agreeable and open

minded, traits which are viewed positively by employers when making hiring decisions.

There are various exercises that you can use to help you self-reflect and support your state of thankfulness:

1. Keep a gratitude journal – small actions over a period of time can have a big impact. Simply writing down a few sentences each day before you practice your visualizations will help you feel more positive, enjoy good experiences, deal better with adversity, and build stronger relationships through your interview process.

2. Embrace your relationships and verbally acknowledge people for their support. Taking the time to tell somehow how grateful you are to have them in your life releases dopamine and serotonin, two hormones that directly relate to your happiness. Feeling positive in your relationships has a direct correlation to your ability to persevere in challenging times, which will help you with your interviews.

3. Remember your past experiences – embrace the bad, reflect on the difficult times which helped prepare you, think about how far you have come in building the life you have. By reflecting on your past, you create a sense of contrast in your mind that enables you to better appreciate positive things in the present.

The benefits of practicing thankfulness and being grateful are numerous. Thankfulness forms a key component of your preparation to interview as it enables your cognitive self to be positively grounded, which will help you to offset negativity, build confidence, and continue to work towards happiness and an ideal interview outcome.

Chapter Summary

There are six key areas involved in building a strong mentality as part of your preparation to interview successfully.

Key Takeaway: Positive preparation for your interview involves understand-ding the time and investment required to seek a new job, trusting and grounding yourself in your planning, applying yourself to address and positively utilize anxiety, physically enabling yourself to succeed, noting and leveraging the fact that you are not alone and have a key support network, and utilizing the power of visualization and thankfulness to drive you forward.

Section 2: External Preparation

Planning for success

Section Introduction

The previous chapters highlighted the importance of mental reflection and mindfulness as a part of interview preparation, enabling you to benefit from both enhanced intrinsic motivation and a stronger mentality. These two outcomes are vital to your internal preparation, grounding you appropriately through your job search and positively influencing the journey ahead.

In the following two chapters we'll shift our focus to external preparation. This is the pre-work which will enable you to showcase to prospective employers not only that you are the best candidate for the job, but that you care, are passionate, are a leader, can make a positive difference, and that you will be around for a long time.

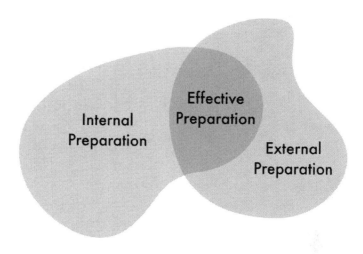

Effective preparation incorporates elements of both internal and external preparation. Both are equally important to your success in interviewing.

Chapter 3: Crafting your resume and cover letter

Think of your resume and corresponding cover letter as the tools that will make a first impression on a prospective employer. Your success in being invited to interview depends largely on this first impression, and it starts by successfully differentiating yourself from the other applicants. Thus, as you seek to gain the opportunity to interview, your overall preparation for each role and interview opportunity should commence with tailoring your resume and cover letter to highlight your skills, experience, developmental potential, and leadership qualities. Note: this is not an exercise in deception. Resume-padding is unethical and counterproductive. Presenting an accurate representation of yourself through your application enables you to shine and articulate your experiences during the interview process. If your resume is a work of fiction, even in part, this will become evident during your interviews when the depth of your answers relating to your magnified experiences lacks breadth and depth. Genuineness is a critical factor for hiring managers in determining a candidate's appropriateness for a role. Be confident in your expertise and experience, and avoid falling into the trap of misrepresenting yourself and wasting your invested time and preparation.

Tailoring your resume for the role

Of course, that doesn't mean you should use the same resume for every application. Adapting your resume to fit the requirements of the specific role you are applying for is essential. Further, tailoring your application sets yourself apart from the large number of standardized resumes that recruiters and hiring managers will receive. As you prepare your resume, aim to highlight your strengths and how you would be a strong match for the particular job you're aiming for.

Some best practices to assist your preparation:

1. Focus on the job description. Use this to understand what an organization and recruiting team is specifically looking for in applicants. Pinpoint any required or desirable skills, knowledge, experience, or qualities.

2. Use this understanding to build out your resume, highlighting specifically the areas where you meet each of the traits the employers are looking for. Through this exercise you will be able to demonstrate how well you fit the role. Be explicit; those reviewing your resume will not assume aspects related to your application that are not communicated.

3. When tailoring the work experience section in your resume, focus on responsibilities which are similar to the job description. Where possible, highlight the objective and measurable positive impact you had relating to these responsibilities. For example, if you were applying for a role of Customer Service Representative and the job advert asked for, "previous experience resolving product and service problems" – you could note that you undertook similar duties in your previous job and consistently provided high level support as demonstrated by your customer satisfaction survey scores (if you have those available). By following this approach, you will separate yourself from other candidates who simply list their duties. Some job seekers like to build this out under a sub section labeled key achievements, which follows each work experience point.

4. The education portion of your resume should list completed course content which aligns with the required knowledge noted within the job posting. If you are currently studying or have partially completed qualifications, it is worthwhile noting when you commenced and your expected completion date, to highlight your ongoing investment in your personal growth and development.

5. Many job seekers include a "Key Skills" section within their resume. Should you include this, ensure you do not simply list your skills but give brief examples of each. For instance, instead of listing, "Ability to lead and motivate teams," further your statement including a sample, e.g., "Ability to lead and motivate teams: Provided clear direction and ongoing support for team members, in person, over the phone and by email on a daily basis. Providing tailored 1-to-1 support leading to an 15% increase in output compared to previous quarter."

6. If you are a recent graduate or just at the beginning of your career, consider making "skills" the focus of your resume and highlighting those you possess, which are transferable to the open role. Skills resumes provide insight into how you have come to possess the skills indicated and highlight examples of how you have used them to achieve an outcome. For example, if applying for a Journalism intern role, content research would be a key skill that could be noted as such: "Research – Able to work with challenging clients in a wide variety of fields. Excellent at researching markets and industries with quick turnaround times and efficiency. Demonstrated through case study analysis projects undertaken as part of MA in Journalism."

7. Once you have updated your experience, education, and skills to align with the requirements of the role, review your personal profile or resume introduction. This is typically a short paragraph that introduces your resume and summarizes your background, knowledge, skills, qualities you will bring, achievements and career goals. Really sell yourself here; be confident in your skills and experience. Example: "A qualified, versatile and passionate

marketing professional with specialized experience in increasing consumer recognition of new entry products. Degree qualified in Marketing. Currently enrolled in MBA and personally focused on increasing strategic thought leadership acumen. Keen interest and career aspirations within social media marketing. Ambition to obtain a position at X organization, where I can further my career for an industry leader that values my experience and leadership skills in managing and motivating creative teams."

Selling yourself with your Cover Letter

While your resume matches your career and skills highlights to the requirements of a role, your cover letter is an opportunity to expand on specific aspects which will distinguish your application. This is an area where you can expand on your strong points, sell them positively, and make a deeper connection with recruiters and hiring managers before they even meet you. Your cover letter should serve as the narrative for your application and include a strong rationale as to how you fit and exceed the hiring criteria as defined by the job posting.

Key elements to incorporate:

1. Ensure you place your name and contact details at the top of your cover letter. While including a postal address is considered overly formal nowadays, you should reference your email and phone number at a minimum.
2. Format your cover letter like a business letter. Include the date below your contact details.
3. Typically, job advertisements will give you insight into who your application should be sent to or who will be reviewing it. Use this information to personally address your application avoiding the use of generic salutations or greetings such as Dear Sir/Madam. If this information is not included, contact the organization via phone or email to understand who you should address your application to. This might seem excessive, but it sets a level of favorable expectation regarding your application and also

demonstrates the degree of detail orientation you are attempting to personify as a professional.

4. Opening paragraph – Make it clear which role you are applying for. You can do this by referencing it as a heading after your greeting line, e.g., "Regarding: Application for Web Developer position" and/or in your opening paragraph e.g., "Dear hiring manager, I am excited to be applying for the recently advertised Web Developer position at X Company." Within your opening, demonstrate your understanding of the organization and that you have a real and genuine interest in joining. Further, to set yourself apart, reference your knowledge of the role/company and where you can add value. For example, if you know the company is focused on increasing its online presence, refer to this and link how your strong technical skills in JavaScript and HTML would provide an advantage in the design and development of online tools.

5. Middle paragraphs - Pick 4-5 desirable skills or experiences that match well with the job description and focus on selling your traits in these areas. Bullet point each and highlight the depth of your skill or experience and how you have used this positively. For example, if the role seeks strong project management skills, articulate where you have demonstrated this and to what effect e.g., "during my time at X organization I was entrusted with managing a range of projects from conception to delivery. Key to my success was my ability to analyze historic data and work collaboratively with other team members to creatively source solutions whilst balancing stakeholder expectations. Through my tact and influence, I was able to increase company savings by 12% through establishing efficient systems of operation and educating targeted team members." This is an example of appropriately utilizing your past experiences and skills to market yourself to a recruiter and hiring manager. Remember, the goal of your cover letter is to ensure that recruiters and hiring managers read your resume. Your ability to highlight how you exemplify key criteria of their job advertisement will ensure you are

considered a strong candidate for the role, enabling you to progress to being shortlisted for an interview. Do not copy your resume verbiage into this section of your cover letter. Re-word the information in your resume, and avoid repeating it. Keep your cover letter short and targeted to the specific points you feel are most important to get across related to your application and let your resume tell the whole story.

6. Closing paragraph – Stay away from long winded cover letter conclusions by ensuring your close is brief and targeted at reiterating that you are thankful for being considered, and that you look forward to discussing your experience and skills in more depth. Sign off sincerely with your name block/digital signature at the bottom.

Taking the time to adapt your cover letter and resume to the role you are applying for is a key aspect of your interview preparation. Beyond differentiating yourself from other candidates and highlighting your strengths, undertaking this process really prepares you for the job in question. By analyzing your experience, education, knowledge, and skills against the requirements of a role, you are able to begin understanding what this

organization values, how this role will help them succeed, and what specifics they are really looking for in the successful candidate. This is key information which you will be able to leverage when you are invited to discuss the role further in an interview.

Cover Letter & Resume best practices

- Keep your cover letter to a single page and your resume to a maximum of two pages. Be concise as you detail your experiences/skills.

- Use the same font and presentation style. Be creative but note that these are professional documents that represent you. Focus on substance, with a design and flow that sets your application apart. If you are applying for a creative/design role, take this opportunity to showcase your skills and talents; this will be expected depending on the industry/roles you are applying for.

- Understand your audience. Mirror language that is used in the job advertisement/posting. Some organizations, such as those within the banking, finance and legal industries, will be more formal in comparison to creative industries or start-up organizations.

- When listing your contact details, ensure that your email reads professionally. It's a good idea to use an email address that's plain and reflects your name (e.g. "bobsmith@gmail.com" versus rocketman@gmail.com).

- If including hyperlinks within your resume to your LinkedIn or to an online website/portfolio of work, ensure that the content is actually up to date and relevant to your application. Double check to ensure that the URL is correct.

- Double and triple check your application for grammatical and spelling errors, focusing on areas such as company name and content. If possible, have a family member or close friend proofread your cover letter and resume to ensure that the content reads well and presents as polished. Seek feedback and redraft any language that is unclear or confusing.

Chapter Summary

Simply put, unless you can make a positive first impression on a recruiter or hiring manager, you won't even get a chance to interview. As such, your external interview preparation must start with a focus on your resume and cover letter. Done well, these documents will help you stand out and lead to the opportunity to further engage with the interview process.

By tailoring your cover letter and resume to the role you are applying for, you have effectively assessed and aligned yourself with the requirements of the position. Should you be invited to interview, this preparation gives you a head start towards understanding requirements such as experience, skills and educational points, which you can further leverage to make yourself shine. For example, if a key focus of the role is driving sales and this is a specific area you have experience in, then you should market this point during live conversations when called to discuss your interest and experience further or when asked to interview in person. Further, by revising your resume, you also become more familiar with it and are better equipped to answer questions related to your overall skills and experience when interviewing.

Admittedly, tailoring your resume and cover letter to each application is time consuming. It is easier to simply provide a standard version of each to prospective employers.

Arguably, you could just focus your efforts on applying for a narrow range of positions, covering more job applications in less time than if you put in the effort to customize your resume and cover letter. This approach however will not get you recognized, nor will it differentiate you from other applicants. Dedication to effective preparation is an example of the standard of commitment you'll need to truly be successful. It will take longer to tailor your resume and cover letter for each job, but doing so will make you a stronger candidate, more likely to land an interview and perform better once you do.

Chapter 4: Continuing your preparation while you wait to hear back

You have done the hard work: you've customized your cover letter and resume for an open position at an organization that really excites you, and now you are waiting to hear back from them. Do not waste this precious time just sitting around waiting! No application comes with the promise of a follow up call from a recruiter or invitation to interview, no matter how great your experience or how well-written your cover letter was. While you are waiting, consider maintaining your momentum by continuing to apply for other jobs that excite you. Follow the same methodological approach to adapting your cover letter and resume to each job description. By applying for more jobs, you continue flexing your mental muscles, reviewing your experience, skills, and expertise against different requirements. Subconsc-iously, each role you apply for by tailoring your cover letter and resume helps you understand your marketable points, strengths, and areas that you can further develop. This data is highly valuable and helps you grow comfortable and more confident in yourself, even before you interview. As with your internal preparation, it is important to continue to ground yourself in the journey at hand and note that each role you apply for is a further opportunity to gain valuable perspective through self-reflection and learning.

While patience is a virtue, following up with an organization that you directly applied with may be beneficial – if done correctly. Most applicants rarely follow up, assuming that if they have not heard back, then they likely have not made the shortlist. This may be true, but you can gain greatly from making contact and reconfirming your keen interest in the job, provided you avoid overwhelming recruiters/hiring managers. Done correctly, this contact creates another positive point of differentiation to enable you to standout against other applicants. Recruiters typically re-review an application when a candidate follows up; it shows that you're serious about applying, and may bump up assessment of your application for shortlisting and initial screening.

Should you not have a direct contact to reach out to, or the job advert/role description did not provide one, try informal channels. LinkedIn works well once you have done your research around who is best to contact and the appropriate timeframe for reaching out. Take into consideration that one to two weeks is typical for recruiters/managers to review applicants for most roles. Keep your message short and summarize your interest and application. For example: "Hi [name], I hope you are well. I recently applied for the X position at X organization. I'm confident my past experience in [insert], and my strong [insert] skills that will make me a valuable asset for the company. Please let me know if you have any questions about my application. I sincerely look forward to hearing from the team and thank you for your consideration."

Chapter Summary

Continuing to apply for roles is an ongoing process and part of your preparation to interview. Continuing to assess yourself against differing criteria for each application enables you to self-reflect and gain confidence with your experience and skills. Should you consider following up with an organization you applied to, be sure to determine the appropriate timing and contact person prior to using the opportunity to reiterate your interest and expertise.

Section 3: Interview Preparation

Section Introduction

As you move to the interactive phases of interviewing – screening interviews and in person/final interviews – your preparation will focus on setting you up for success by building further upon both internal (mentality) and external (connection) elements you have established. The following two chapters cover typical timelines, touchpoints in a typical interview process, and what you can do to ground yourself and prepare purposefully to leave a memorable impression, distinguishing yourself from all the other applicants and maximizing your chances of success.

Chapter 5: Sailing through the screening interview

An initial phone or screening interview highlights that you have been flagged as an individual who fits the broad criteria for an open role. It is a significant milestone on the pathway to being hired into your dream job, and it highlights that your preparation, both internal and external, is paying off. For context, for many positions at large organizations, typically only 15% of candidates receive a phone interview, and only a third of these individuals are shortlisted to progress to in-person interviews. It is worth noting that the goal of phone/screening interviews is to assess your presentability for the next round and to discuss specific aspects of your resume related to how your experience and skills match against the role requirements, competencies, and required knowledge. To be successful, you have to be prepared to present yourself in the best light possible on that phone call.

The initial contact

Recruiters and hiring managers will typically reach out to you via email or LinkedIn to set up a phone/screening interview. Reply in a courteous and professional manner, aiming to set up a time where you will be able to fully engage with the process. In some instances, unscheduled calls are made to candidates, with the intent of assessing how you react in unplanned circumstances. Should you receive one of these calls, politely schedule an alternative time to talk. Being fully prepared is key. Even if you are confident in your knowledge of the role and your application, it pays for you to buy yourself some time to enable yourself to strategically prepare to present yourself in the most positive light. To do this, say something to the effect of, "I really appreciate your time, but I'm not in a private space right now and won't be able to give this call the attention it deserves. Can we set up an alternate time to connect?" Recognize that this is a time-sensitive process for recruiters and hiring managers, so set up a call back for the following day if you can; this gives you an evening to prepare.

It is critically important that you have a professional-sounding voicemail set up. You could miss an incoming call or not be able to answer. From the moment you begin applying for open jobs, you should expect to begin receiving calls from potential employers. Your voicemail is a point of interaction and makes an impression on the individual calling. Do not stand out for the wrong reasons. Recruiters and hiring managers have been known to drop a candidate from consideration following an interaction with a novelty or joke voicemail message.

Groundwork for a successful screening interview

All your preparation to date has led you to this point. Channel your excitedness and inner motivation into your planning to set yourself up for success.

Compare your resume to the job advertisement/job description. When you applied for the role and tailored your cover letter and resume as part of your application, you should have noted key areas where your experience and skills aligned with the job description. Reflect on these areas and be prepared to talk to these during your phone interview. You want to create common ground as a way to bond with the recruiter or hiring manager and so creating these connections between your skills and experience and what they are looking for within the role is a key aspect in your success.

One of the key advantages you have in the phone /screening interview is that you can prepare your notes and be in the comfort of your own environment. To this point, plan to have a copy of the job advertisement and your application in front of you when you connect with the recruiter/hiring manager. As part of your preparation, highlight areas for you to reference during your conversation. During the phone/screening interview, it's important to actively listen and to respond succinctly. Overselling yourself by dominating the conversation won't be viewed positively. By drawing parallels between your application and the role ahead of time, you will be prepared to engage more naturally. You may be asked specific questions; alternatively, you may be given the opportunity to discuss your application openly. In each case, follow the rationale of highlighting your relevant experience, discussing what you did, and the positive impacts. For example, "thanks for the added context/I feel I can relate to this through my experience, we had a similar situation at ABC company. I was responsible for [insert] and achieved X favorable outcome by [insert process/methods you used]."

Plan to take your screening interview in a quiet setting with no distractions.

Brainstorming your past success

Through your inner preparation up to this point you have reflected in detail around your career to date. Use these reflections to think through your success stories and how you can communicate these as a response to any questions that may be asked during your phone /screening interview. Rehearse your stories, aiming to keep each to 30 seconds or less. Use the job advertisement/role description to educate yourself as to likely questions in this space. For example, if stakeholder management is listed as a core competency, you will probably get a question about communication and balancing priorities. Think through and write down your personal wins in relation to each key criterion so you have these in front of you during you call and can elaborate as needed. This approach will also assist you in concisely answering any behavioral or experience type questions that you may be asked (we'll cover this more in the coming chapters).

It pays to research

At some point, most likely early in the conversation, you will probably be asked the following questions: Why are you leaving your current position? Why do you want to join our company? What do you know of the organization? What interests you in the role?

As part of your interview notes, have a prepared response to these questions reflecting on both your personal circumstances and understanding of the job and organization. Avoid mentioning that you are seeking greater compensation or benefits; instead, address these questions with goals that you are looking to achieve in regard to your career. Aligning yourself with a market leader to drive your career development or picking up responsibilities and heightened job duties are positive examples of how you can plan to respond. Be strategic and prepare for these questions by diving into recent company news, their website, and social media accounts so you can really present yourself as someone who identifies with the organization. By doing your homework on the company's products and services before you interview, you will pinpoint areas you can bring up in conversation. Note that your interviewer is not only assessing your overall fit for the role, but also your ability to align with and add to company mission, values, and culture. Plan to use this opportunity to showcase your eagerness and understanding of the organization and your own connection with the product and/or service the company offers.

Further, while it may not be allowable for a recruiter or hiring manager to explicitly ask you what your current salary is (depending on state laws), be prepared to engage in some conversation about your salary expectations. Approach your preparation for this in a similar way, by researching the market and knowing the worth of your experience and skills by looking at similar organizations. Websites such as glassdoor.com and payscale.com can provide highly valuable information that will enable you to get a sense of what is typical for a specific group of employers or industry. Use this information to reconcile and understand how much pay you want and need. As it relates to addressing the question of salary expectations, strategically answer the question by asking for the salary range for the position. You can facilitate this by stating something to the effect of, "That is a great question—it would be helpful if you could share what the range is for this position." This approach enables you to collect valuable data and position yourself for future negotiation. Once the recruiter or hiring manager answers, should this range be at or above a level you feel is fair, you can confirm that this works for you by stating, "That is in line with my expectations given my experience and skills." Should the range be lower then you would like, you have a decision to make about your overall involvement moving forward. Be rational and remain engaged. It is still highly valuable experience to continue through the interview process to strengthen your overall confidence, and there will be a formal opportunity to negotiate salary should you be offered the job. In this instance you should answer transparently by stating something like, "Given my experience and skills, I was personally hoping for something in the range of [Insert $ amount - $ amount, annually]. With that being said, finding the right organization and role is the primary goal for me. I'd be happy to revisit compensation at the right time in the future if applicable." This approach enables you to formulate a stronger plan as well as find our more in the meantime about the organization, including benefits and perks which make up its total compensation package. Remember, this is not the time to negotiate, but rather an opportunity to showcase your maturity and poise. Provided you are not worlds apart in your salary expectations and you beat out all competition for the role, you will be in a good position to revisit this.

Don't sell yourself short, know your worth by researching the market

Differentiate yourself from other candidates

Prepare some questions ahead of time as you certainly will be given the opportunity to layer these into the conversation. These should be related directly to the role and/or in relation to the broader organization. Your aim in asking questions should be to showcase why you are a great fit for the role. Ask questions which highlight your understanding of the organization and which you can use to show off your strengths. For example:

- I enjoy working collaboratively and being able to create positive outcomes. Can you tell me more about the team I would be working with and their collective goals?
- I read on the company website/news that [insert positive statistic i.e. market growth or achievement] can you tell me what the key focus areas are strategically for the company moving forward and how this role will help achieve success in these areas?
- I appreciate being able to drive my career development through the work that I do. I'm actively looking for a role that can

support my continuous growth, are you able to talk to me about how the organization encourages the ongoing development of its team members?

- Further, plan to ask questions that will give you a realistic job preview of the role for your own benefit. Recruiters and hiring managers can only communicate so much within a role advert/job description and it is important that you understand the broader context, operating structure, team, and primary purpose to ensure you are a good personal fit. These types of considered questions will also be viewed positively by those interviewing you and will add to the perception that you are a valuable, highly skilled resource who is looking to make a strong impact. Additionally, it is worthwhile to check that your perception of the role aligns with the actual job duties and responsibilities. At times organizations can unintentionally mislead candidates through vague or inaccurate verbiage in their adverts and job descriptions. These questions add to how you come across in terms of confidence and maturity. Remember, interviewing is partially about presenting yourself positively, but it's also collecting data for yourself to ensure this organization and role is the right fit for you. Some questions you could ask for example:

- Is this a new role or replacing an outgoing employee? – gives you information around the intent of your role, primary focus areas and expected impact.

- Can you confirm who is the hiring manager and their title, can you tell me a bit about the teams they manage and their number of direct reports? – provides context around seniority of your direct manager, level of personal support and autonomy in your role.

- Specific questions related to roles and responsibilities as noted in the role advert or job description i.e. collaborative scope, key stakeholders, cross functional aspects.

Your environment

One of the key benefits to a phone/screening interview is that you control the environment in which you are in. Do everything you can to "feel at home" by shutting out distractions and eliminating background noise. Drink some water prior to the call and plan to have a glass on hand. If you have not spoken much through the day, warm up your vocal cords by rehearsing some of your career highlights that you plan to share with the recruiter or hiring manager. To help you settle in, arrive to your space early – 15 minutes prior is ideal so you can set up your notes and review your resume next to the job description. Have a pen and paper ready so you can take any notes that you feel would be useful to reflect on for the in-person interview phase, for example, information about internal projects, work streams, and job/team specific goals that your interviewer might share.

Video conference screening interview Vs. phone interview

More and more organizations are utilizing video conferencing as part of the screening process and so your first interview may be a video call as opposed to a phone interview. Don't worry if this is the case; your preparation process as outlined above remains unchanged, and you have the benefit of being able to utilize visual cues to make a positive impact on your recruiter/hiring manager. To this point, ensure that you have a professionally presentable space to take the video call from, removing anything within web-camera view that would be a distraction or out of place in a professional setting. Resist the urge to take a video call from your car using your mobile device; while this may be an effective way to manage time if you are working, it isn't professional, nor does it allow you enough space to set out your notes and other materials.

Plan to take some time off to take this call from your home. Since you want to present yourself as professionally as possible, dress appropriately. Taking the time and effort to take care of these details is always acknowledged by recruiters and highlights your commitment to the organization and role.

Your preparation for a screening interview should be the same regardless of whether it is a video conference call or a phone interview. For either, since you are in your space, you should be comfortable and benefit from having your notes to refer to. Remember, with video interviewing, you have the addition of visual cues; you are able to leverage this to connect with the recruiter/hiring manager. Look directly at the camera when speaking and smile regularly when conversing as you aim to make a meaningful connection. Avoid focusing on other elements in the room that may take away from your overall positiveness and make it seem like you are disengaged or unsure of yourself.

Of course, life will continue around your interview schedule. You may have parents, roommates, pets, or immediate family members around when you are scheduled to interview. In line with the concept of togetherness covered in chapter 2, lean on them to support you during this time by asking them to limit noises and distractions while you interview. This will ensure you have a quiet space that will be uninterrupted during the interview process, enabling you to focus.

If your screening interview is via video conference, embrace your ability to utilize visual ques to make a positive impression and create rapport with your interviewer.

The mindset you have

Approach your screening interview with the mentality of listening first, with the aim of processing what is being discussed, before responding. The recruiter/hiring manager will be focused on setting the stage, talking about expectations and what qualities the successful candidate will possess. Let them do so and take notes where applicable. Embracing the mindset of an active listener will enable you to come back to these points as necessary when it is your turn to engage.

Your mental state should be one of happiness and enthusiasm. After all, this interview is an amazing opportunity and highlights the progress you have made through your preparation.

One great way to channel this (in particular, if you don't have visuals to create a strong connection with your interviewer) is to smile as you speak when asking questions or discussing your experience and skills. This approach is a technique that ensures your positive feeling towards the process. It also ensures that you project enthusiasm and warmth to the recruiter, positively influencing how they view your overall interaction.

Channeling your enthusiasm for the job will go a long way towards making a favorable impression on both recruiters and hiring managers. Those making the hiring decisions will naturally gravitate towards someone who really wants to join their team. Be aware that this should not come across as over eagerness, but if this is a dream job or significant career move, you should want this enthusiasm to shine through all of your interactions. Listen intently, follow the conversation, and ask considered questions related to the discussion (and your research). These are all ways you can naturally enable your enthusiasm to shine through and impact how you are perceived positively.

Your mental state during your screening interview should reflect happiness and enthusiasm.

End positively

You've had a great conversation and remain interested in the job and organization. How you end your interview gives you an opportunity to express this and enhance your image of professionalism. Thank the interviewer for their time, reiterate that you appreciated the insights about the role and remain extremely interested in joining the organization. Ask what the next steps will be and that you look forward to meeting them in person.

Later in the day, reinforce your gratitude with a thank you note emailed to your interviewer. Let a few hours go by before you send this. Reiterate these points: thankfulness for being able to discuss the role further; links between your experience and role requirements from your conversation, and the fact that you remain very interested and look forward to hearing from them regarding next steps. Keep this message concise, remembering that this is a professional courtesy; you have already sold yourself within the interview.

Reflection & refinement

The screening interview process should have given you valuable insight into the organization, its culture, and expectations for the job. From your interaction and questions asked, you should walk away understanding the key areas a hiring manager is looking for from a successful candidate and challenges faced. Take some time following your interview to reflect on what you learned. Did it seem as though your interviewer was asking questions focused on particular themes, e.g. collaboration and teamwork, working with challenging stakeholders, communication? If so, this is valuable information which you should prepare to elaborate on, should you be invited to the next stage of in person interviews.

Think through how you performed. Remember, interviewing is a journey and those that do it best prepare both internally and externally at a high level and aim to learn from each opportunity. To help you reflect, ask yourself the following questions:

- Was I concise in my messaging when asked about my career to date?
- Did I highlight my skills and experience to draw connections to the job requirements?
- Were my questions about the role, job description and my research well received?
- Was I relaxed and confident? Did the interviewer walk away with a favorable impression of me?

Resist the urge to be overly critical of yourself. Your self-reflection is aimed at understanding areas that you can further develop. It is a positive process and not one where you should ridicule yourself.

Trust in your preparation to date. Remain patient; you will know soon enough if you are progressing to the next round; if this position was not to be, you can take what you've learned and focus on other jobs.

Chapter Summary

Your internal and external preparation has led you to being selected for a screening interview. To continue your upward trajectory and move onto the next phase of the recruitment process - in person interviews, focus your preparation on understanding the cross section of role requirements V your experience and skillset. Reflect by reviewing your resume and past experiences and prepare to concisely discuss them. Focus on connecting with your interviewer through the phone or video call, and prepare questions which highlight your strengths and demonstrate your aptitude, understanding, and enthusiasm. Ensure that your physical location sets you up for success by enabling you to be comfortable and relaxed going into your screening interview.

Chapter 6: Acing the in-person/final interviews

The process of interviewing is a journey with one winner: the successful candidate. Your internal and external preparation as outlined in this book has provided you with a platform to elevate yourself. However, you and you alone, have achieved this, thanks to your time, effort, dedication, self-reflection, mindfulness, and consistency. You have been asked to interview in person, the culmination of your journey so far. You have successfully navigated the initial phases of recruitment and outperformed others in being shortlisted to interview. Up to this point you have analyzed the job description against your experience, studied the organizations culture and values, gained insight into the specifics of the role, and pinpointed key areas you can positively impact. At this point, how you present yourself in person and project your experience and skills will be the determining factors in your ability to receive an offer of employment for your dream job. Simply put, you should know what to expect thanks to your screening interviews and interactions and through all of your reflections and preparation to this point. Now it's simply about putting all the pieces together. You have the insights, tools and knowledge required to successfully interview.

This concluding part of your journey is about final touches, maintaining your poise, and presentation skills. In this chapter, we will walk through each of the key areas of in person interviews to enable you to pull all of your preparation up to this point together and to put your best foot forward and truly separate yourself from the competition. The chapter is chronologically ordered and split into four areas:

1. Pre-interview planning and factfinding
2. Night before the interview
3. Day of the interview
4. Post interview

Pre-Interview planning and factfinding

Your interview agenda

If the recruiter or hiring manager has not provided you with an agenda for your in- person interview, politely ask them for an outline or overview. Understanding the agenda is a vital first step in your preparation and highlights aspects such as who you will be meeting and interviewing with from the organization, expected timing, the interview structure, and any other expectations they may have. Some agendas also provide useful information such as building access, parking instructions, and sign-in details.

Think of the agenda as a guide to what your day will look like. Pay attention to the information it contains, and use it to your benefit to assist your preparation.

In analyzing your agenda, review who will be interviewing you. Use LinkedIn and the organizations website to learn more about who these individuals are. They might be potential team members, the manager who the job reports to, or upper level executives who you might interface with should you be successful in joining the organization. Understanding with whom you will be interviewing with is critical to understanding the types of questions you will be asked and the likely expectations of your interviewer so you can prepare appropriately. For example, a team member will likely value communication and collaboration skills, vetting your overall fit for the team from an organizational culture perspective. A hiring manager will likely look to assess your expertise, judgment, and technical skills to ensure you can perform the core functions of the role. Understanding who is who in your interview agenda enables you to reflect on how you will approach each conversation and what connections you will look to make. In addition, research the organization to understand if there have been any recent announcements or company news since your screening interview. Take this as an opportunity to showcase how much of a good fit you are and how invested you are in the organization. Those interviewing you will see this favorably, in particular if you can leverage your understanding of current events and effectively bring these into your discussions with each individual.

Related to the interview structure, it's important to understand whether your interview will be set up for one-on-one style conversations or group/panel interviews with multiple stakeholders involved at one time. Avoid being blindsided by an arrangement you weren't expecting. If there isn't any information about the interview structure, it would be worth talking to the recruiter or hiring manager to gain more insight, enabling you to prepare effectively. Should you be set up for group or panel interviews, ensuring you know the job title and background of each member is essential to interviewing well in this setting allowing you to engage and create a meaningful connection with each individual appropriately. If the agenda indicates that you will be expected to undertake a case study analysis or technical assessment as part of your interview, you will be able to effectively brush up on these skills and hone them ahead of time. Leveraging online modules and working through examples is a good way to effectively prepare if this kind of assessment is part of the organization's interview expectations of you.

We covered the power of visualization in section 1. If this resonated with you, use the mental rehearsal technique discussed to picture yourself making a positive impression on each interviewer in line with the flow of your agenda. Visualizing a positive performance will offset any anxiety, while further increasing your connection to your desired behavior and outcomes.

Reflect on your past interactions

By now, you've had various conversations with the recruiter/hiring manager. Take the time to go over your notes from these conversations, and reflect on what types of questions were asked of you and what content was discussed. Prepare to revisit these topics again during your in-person interview and aim to be able to have a more in-depth conversation. Think through how you plan to ask articulate and thoughtful questions about these topics, should the opportunity present itself. Finally, refresh yourself on the job advertisement and role description so you can tie conversations back to key criteria that your interviewers will be measuring you up against.

Think about your story

Successful candidates have a strong overall narrative/story, which they use to build rapport with interviewers. A common question used as an icebreaker is often some variation of "tell me about yourself." It is vitally important that you can answer this question without recounting your whole life story and personal milestones. Your aim here should be to succinctly sum up why you are an ideal candidate and are suited for the role as well as why you want the job. This is your chance to lead the conversation and make an ideal first impression, so take the time to prepare your elevator pitch. Build a narrative around your relevant skills, strengths, areas of specialization, and expertise. If you are a new graduate or new to the workforce you can focus on your education and your passions for your field of study along with your future ambitions. Irrespective of your experience level, mention your focus on career growth and increasing responsibilities; these are always looked upon favorably and position you as a driven, development-focused individual. Finish up by summarizing why the organization appeals to you. Remember, be detailed but succinct; you want to pique the interest of the interviewer and overall make a positive impression. Prepare your narrative and practice it. Note that you can adapt your answer to other questions such as "why this company?" or "why this role?"

Strategize your responses to questions

The most common interview questions asked typically center around understanding your strengths and weaknesses. You may be asked to explicitly state what these are, from your perspective. As such you should prepare these in advance. Use the following guidelines to prepare and structure your response:

- For your strengths, align these with specific skills that can be backed up through experience. This doesn't have to be corporate experience, but align your example with the role you are interviewing for. For example, if you plan to respond with communication skills, think through an example you could use to highlight how you leveraged this strength to solve a problem or navigate a tough situation. Resist the urge to waffle or be modest when discussing your strengths; you do not want to sell yourself short but being over eager here will come across as overbearing and conceited.

- For your weaknesses, tread carefully. It is important to be honest; however ground yourself in self-development and do not overshare. For example, if listing a hard skill, such as creating pivot tables and reports in Micosoft Excel or Google Sheets, reiterate your desire to actively address by noting a class or course you are currently taking. If listing a soft skill such as giving presentations/public speaking, highlight your developmental plans and steps you have taken to improve yourself. Highlighting your investment in improvement is key here, and will make a positive impression even if your skill in this area isn't where you want it to be.

- In addition, you will likely be asked both behavioral and situational questions by your interviewers.
- Behavioral questions are those that interviewers ask to gain insight into what you have done or would do in certain circumstances and how you think. In particular, interviewers use these questions to gain an understanding of your problem-solving skills. Typically, these questions challenge an individual to recall a difficult or challenging situation experienced previously and how a positive outcome was achieved. An example of a behavioral interview question would be, "tell me about a time where you used your problem-solving skills to help drive a project to completion."
- Situational questions are hypothetical "what if" questions which aim to highlight your ability to think on your feet by asking you to assess a situation and describe how you would handle/resolve. An example of a situational question would be, "how would you prioritize multiple projects with conflicting deadlines?"

There is a science behind your preparation to answer these types of questions. Overall, the key is not to rehearse and memorize your statements, but rather to develop a general strategy through an understanding of your career experiences to date and being able to adapt them to answer questions on the fly.

Your ability to develop compelling stories is key to your preparation to effectively answer behavioral and situational questions. As part of this process, reflect on challenging circumstances you have encountered and overcome at work. If you are a recent graduate, new to the job market, follow the same process but think about comparable experiences you've encountered during your studies, team sport interactions, or at college/university. Your aim here is to have 5-7 examples which you can adapt to the question being asked, highlighting how you were able to react, gain a positive outcome, and achieve a milestone or goal. The best candidates reflect on both their resume and the job description here and tie back their experiences specifically to key aspects of the role being interviewed for. Use your previous interactions and time already spent understanding the job description to your advantage by thinking through the types of behavioral questions they could ask related to role needs as well as your specific experience.

An example of this would be having multiple examples that demonstrate high level communication and stakeholder management skills. When asked the question, "tell me about a time when team members disagreed with you on a key project and how you went about gaining agreement," you will be able to use an example which demonstrates your experience and your thought process, further explaining how you achieved a positive outcome.

Behavioral and Situational interview questions typically fall into ten key areas.

Review each against your experiences and career to date to assist your preparation:

1. Teamwork

    *   Example question: We have all made mistakes that we wish we could take back. Tell me about a time you wish you had managed a situation another way with a colleague.

2. Client facing skills

    *   Example question: How do you go about prioritizing the needs of your customers'?

3. Ability to adapt

    *   Example question: Describe a time when your team or organization was undergoing some change. How did this impact your role and deliverables, and how did you adapt to the situation?

4. Time management

   - Example question: Tell me about a time in which you had to be strategic in order to meet all your top priorities.

5. Communication:

   - Example question: Give me an example of a time when you had to explain something fairly complex to a frustrated and combative stakeholder who disagreed with you. How did you handle this fragile situation and drive your interaction towards a favorable conclusion?

6. Motivation and Value

   - Example question: Give me an example of a time you were able to think outside the box and get creative with your work. Did you enjoy this? What aspects were difficult about it?

7. Problem solving

   - Example question: Describe an instance when you used your problem-solving skills to the benefit of your team.

8. Failure

   - Example question: Tell me about a decision that you have made and regretted on a key project or work product and how you overcame it.

9. Leadership

   - Example question: Give me an example of when you delegated work across an entire team. Related to this, how did you go about defining roles and responsibilities?

10. Personal Stress

- Example question: Tell me about a time you worked well under pressure. What did you learn about yourself through this experience?

Additionally, prepare by reviewing each of your experience points in your resume. You should expect interviewers to dive into these by asking both behavioral and situational questions to test your abilities in each area listed. Mentally rehearse talking about specific achievements, working to describe each concisely and effectively. A technique which may help provide you with a structure to build your answers is known as the STAR framework, standing for Situation, Task, Action and Results. When rehearsing your answers, plan to cover each of these points.

Situation	Task	Activity	Result
Set the scene	What was your responsibility?	What did you do?	How did the situation end?

1. Situation – Provide a brief recount of the context for the task, project or challenge faced. Be specific.
2. Task – Describe your role and responsibilities overall as they related to the situation.
3. Action – Highlight how you went about completing the task or dealing with the challenge. Articulate what you did specifically or what you were able to lead the team to achieve. Avoid focusing on what your coworkers did or what your manager directed you to do, and focus primarily on your actions.
4. Result – Explain the value-added outcomes and positive results achieved by your work and actions. Emphasize your accomplishments as well as what your learned and took away from the experience.

Overall, the STAR framework enables you to answer both behavioral and situational interview questions by helping you structure your answers into when, where, what, and how, and allows you to discuss results while avoiding repetition and waffling.

Night before the interview

Revisit how far you have come

When you initially started preparing for the interview process, you grounded yourself with some key motivation and mentalities. These included navigating your intrinsic values, wants and needs, and embracing concepts of togetherness and thankfulness, attentiveness, and focus, and addressing anxiety. As you look forward to tomorrow's interview, revisit all of these concepts and your preparation. This will heighten your sense of self confidence related to all you have achieved to this point. Indeed, to get to where you are now, you have already evolved as an individual and likely applied yourself in ways you had not before. It's not quite time to celebrate yet, but taking a moment to acknowledge your accomplishments will reinforce your own positivity and focus during your final push.

Plan what you will wear

Set out your clothes for your interview, with the aim of dressing professionally. Note that what is considered professional attire varies per industry and organization. It's a good idea to dress one level above the organization's status quo. You can figure this out by looking through the company website, media releases, and social media posts to get a feel for the corporate culture and how you can present yourself appropriately. Remember that what you wear will be a part of the overall impression you will make; avoid bold colors and patterns or making a fashion statement. You want to be remembered as being well-presented and polished, not outlandish.

Your clothing is a reflection of what you represent. Take your time to think about how you want to present to further your image of professionalism.

Review logistics

Plan your route to the interview ahead of time. Allow plenty of extra time for traffic or unforeseen circumstances, especially if you choose to take public transit to your interview location. Overall, you want to arrive early enough to give yourself some time to review your notes and to acquaint yourself with your surroundings.

The time you spend planning before you commute is important. The fewer things you need to figure out on the actual day of your interview, the better.

It is also worthwhile to think about your pre-interview meals. After all, you do not want hunger pangs impacting your performance ability. Aim to eat two to three hours before your interview. More than likely, this will be breakfast or lunch so plan ahead. Keep it simple; now is not the time to try new foods or cuisines. Stick with something that you eat with some regularity, which is ideally light and nutritious.

Remember how you choose to fuel yourself for your interview will set up your performance. Don't go overboard with caffeine and carbohydrates; you want to feel full of energy, not weighed down and lethargic.

Read over your notes

Up to this point you have compiled numerous notes for your various interactions with the recruiting process. You should feel strongly encouraged by the fact that you have armed yourself with everything you need for your upcoming interview. Do one final review of your notes in the evening prior to bed.

Focus on your narrative/story, how your resume experience and skills compare with the job advert/description, and your pre planned questions/conversation points for each person interviewing you. Remember – you are simply reviewing at this point. The interview is going to center on the topic which you know best: yourself. You have done a great deal of preparation and have a great advantage. Use this time to go over your details so they remain fresh within your mind.

Visualization

It's completely natural to feel some form of nervousness or anxiety the night before your interview. Offset this by visualizing positive imagery related to your interview success. Envision yourself creating an instant connection with each interviewer and providing clear, concise, and articulate responses to their questions, and receiving positive feedback at the conclusion of the interview. Use positive affirmations in the form of self-talk to tell yourself that you are well-prepared and will do very well the following day in your conversations, highlighting your strengths and outshining all others.

Of course, you don't have to wait until the night before your interview to benefit from the positivity of visualization. As highlighted within chapter two, as part of your internal preparation and focus on building a strong mentality, you can harness the power of visualization to build your confidence and to overcome stress and anxiety.

Go over this content one more time; consider making this part of your daily routine if you have not already. The more you practice visualization, the more benefit you will get out of it.

Sleep

Ensuring you get enough sleep the night before your interview is critical. Most individuals require 6-8 hours of uninterrupted sleep to be their best. Aim for what works for you. Avoid oversleeping and starting your day behind schedule by setting two different alarms for the morning.

If you are struggling to get to sleep and find yourself fixated on your upcoming interview, consider using breathing exercises to help put you in a state of calmness. The 4-7-8 breathing technique involves breathing in for 4 seconds, holding your breath for 7 seconds, and then exhaling for 8 seconds; this often works to alleviate anxiety.

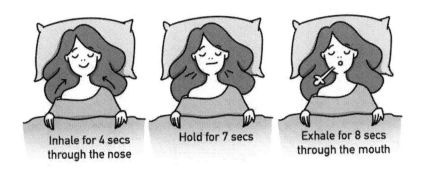

Inhale for 4 secs through the nose   Hold for 7 secs   Exhale for 8 secs through the mouth

The 4-7-8 technique helps to put you in 'rest and digest mode' by triggering your parasympathetic nervous system which lowers your blood pressure and promotes sleep.

The interview day

Morning of your interview

Your morning routine should be optimized so you can walk into your interview confident, fresh, and sharp. As you wake up, remember that you have prepared both internally and externally more intensively than any other candidate. Center yourself in this fact while you get ready. Before you leave home, pack your notes and be sure to do one final check of the organization's website, social media, and news so you can be aware of any breaking events, such as new product launches or company expansions. You will be able to reference this information within your interview interactions.

Consider scheduling a morning workout to boost your energy levels, clear your mind, and help you feel focused. A core benefit of exercising in the morning is that it ties into your positive psychology; by accomplishing something beneficial before the day truly begins, you prime yourself for further achievements and success through the momentum you have created.

No matter what, eat your planned meal, especially if your interview is mid-morning or before lunch. You might feel like skipping breakfast, but this is not a good idea: you want your blood sugar levels to be at their optimum and not negatively impact you during the interview.

If you do not have time for a workout, going for a walk to get some fresh air and sunshine can provide similar benefits and a great boost of natural energy.

Your arrival

Note that your interview actually begins the moment you enter the vicinity of the interview office/location, including when you drive into the parking lot or walk into the building. Be switched on for this –do not wait until the first questions from your interviewer(s) to embrace and showcase your pleasant and professional demeanor. This is important, as you never know who may be present in the greeting/reception area, who you might share an elevator ride with, or who you parked next to. Each interaction could potentially be with someone who is a key decision maker or has some influence on the overall hiring process, so ensure you are present and alert. Treat every single person with whom you interact as someone who might have a say in whether or not to hire you. Aim to be warm and professional with everyone you interact with from the moment you arrive.

Plan to arrive at your interview location 20-30 minutes ahead of schedule. Remain in your car or find a quiet location where you can center yourself, calm any nerves, and review your notes one last time. Before you head to the reception area to check in, close your eyes, take some deep breaths, and visualize your successful interview. Check your physical appearance in a mirror or with your phone to make sure you are neat and professional. If you have any anxiousness, mentally reconcile this as excitement; after all, the moment you have long been preparing for is finally here.

As you approach the building, turn your phone off or to airplane mode. Avoid just keeping it on silent; those interviewing you will still hear the vibrations of a missed call or notifications, and it may interrupt the flow of your discussions. Upon arrival at the greeting/reception area, introduce yourself to the receptionist, if one is present (this process may be automated with an electronic guest sign in). Let them know who you are scheduled to meet with, per your agenda. Note that some organizations may have you sign confidentiality and non-disclosure agreements before proceeding to the interview. If so, this typically will be taken care of during the check-in process. If following check-in you are asked to take a seat in the waiting area, use the time to focus on your mental calmness. Take a few deep breaths and relax. This is not the time for reviewing notes or trying to mentally rehearse your speaking points. Trust in your preparation; it got you this far. Take in your surroundings and be at peace. If you absolutely must keep yourself busy, then note that most organizations keep publications referencing their work, services or products on hand as reading material. Flicking through this content can give you valuable further insight into the organization. However, if you do decide to do this, don't get too engrossed in your reading – be mindful that you will be interrupted shortly. The last thing you want is to seem startled and flustered when you are taken to the interview area.

When the time arrives, greet your interviewer with eye contact and a firm handshake and introduce yourself. As you make your way to the interview, be ready to engage in small talk; do not overdo your engagement here, or you risk coming across as nervous and talkative. Best practice would be to follow the lead of your interviewer and let them establish the direction of the discussion. If you come across something of note on route to the interview room/area, use your personal link to it to discuss your shared interest which you can use to establish a heightened connection, e.g. artwork you recognize or sports memorabilia that might adorn the walls.

The interview – body language and nonverbal positioning

As you walk into the interview room, remember to be yourself; relax and breathe. The person interviewing you is a key decision maker and potentially your future manager, but they are a person and just like you they have good days and bad days and a life outside of work. Remember your aim is to have a positive discussion and to make a strong human connection.

Note that when you engage in conversation, your voice and responses will reflect your feelings. When you are relaxed, your vocal cords produce lower, more natural notes. Being stressed, on the other hand, pushes your voice to a higher pitch, often coming across as more raspy. Research has shown that those with lower pitched speech are viewed as more authoritative and certain, and this is the outcome you are seeking. By being relaxed you not only enable yourself to better convey your experience, skills and desire for the role, but you enable yourself to use your voice and speech habits to influence your interviewer's perception of you. For this same reason, when talking, be mindful of how fast you are speaking and remember to slow your answers down. Fast speakers are difficult to follow and come across as anxious and nervous. Use silence to your advantage here when you structure your answers and responses. Pause before you begin to answer any questions and when reiterating your experience and skills, ensure you take a brief break at the end of each sentence. Using periods of silence may seem awkward, but it comes across as calculated and thoughtful; when discussing lengthy parts of your story, your interviewer will appreciate the time it gives them to process what you are saying.

Your posture is also important. Human communication theory suggests that your body language makes up between 50-60% of your overall communication[7]. As such, you need to be aware of your posture and nonverbal cues. If you are meeting with multiple interviewers, stand and shake hands when each enters the room, if within close proximity. This gesture brings you to the same level physically as your interviewer, a subconscious move that creates a feeling of neutrality which is beneficial in setting the scene for the interview and imminent conversations.

Position yourself directly opposite from your interviewer and adjust your chair if necessary, so that your eye level is similar. Positioning yourself in this way subconsciously shows that you are confident and open to engaging. When seated, sit slightly forward in your chair and ensure you keep your posture upright with your chin up and shoulders down. This projects enthusiasm and indicates that you're highly engaged in the conversation at hand. Slouching back in your chair with poor posture makes you seem unfocused, unfriendly, and disengaged.

When conversing, feel free to use your hands to talk if this is natural to you, but avoid rapid movements and excessive gesturing that will distract from your statements. As you complete your response or when you are actively listening, place your hands on the table in a neutral open position. This posture demonstrates that you have nothing to hide and are confident. Avoid crossing your arms, as this is often interpreted as a defensive posture. Place your feet in comfortable position through the interview, but avoid crossing your legs at the knee or placing an ankle over one knee. These positions make it difficult to lean forward and engage, and limit your ability to sit facing your interviewer. The most neutral position is with your feet flat on the ground.

Also, remember that you may be sitting for a while; crossing your feet at the ankle may become uncomfortable mid-way through the interview, and having to move them can distract from the conversation. Be mindful and do what works best for you.

---

[7] Cummings, K (2011) Nonverbal Communication and First Impressions, Kent State University Honors College:
https://etd.ohiolink.edu/apexprod/rws_etd/send_file/send?accession=ksuhonors130516
1866&disposition=inline

Sit upright & lean slightly forward

Maintain an open posture

Be comfortable

Keep your feet flat on the ground

Your posture is a key part of your overall body language. Note these principals.

Eye contact is associated with trustworthiness and is a key component of your nonverbal communication. Presentation theory indicates that to make a positive connection, you should make eye contact about 50-70% of the time you are actively communicating[8]. This may seem excessive to you, given that average adults tend to look directly at each other when talking only between 30 and 60% of the time. Use 6-10 second intervals of eye contact, taking regular and persistent breaks to shift your gaze slightly before returning, to ensure your level of eye contact is not viewed as overly intense. It is natural to shift your focus and gaze when thinking through how to respond to a question, and this is expected. When preparing to answer ensure that you shift your focus back upon the interviewer and continue utilizing the interval approach.

Should you be interviewing in a panel setting or with multiple individuals in the room at the same time, be sure to share your gaze with each individual as you communicate before turning your gaze back to the individual asking the question as you conclude your response. Avoid solely focusing upon

[8] Schulz, J (2012) Eye Contact: Don't make these mistakes, Michigan State Extension: https://www.canr.msu.edu/news/eye_contact_dont_make_these_mistakes

the individual asking the questions and regularly scan the room; you want to establish a connection with each stakeholder. Use subtle head nods to demonstrate active listening, enthusiasm, and engagement during questions and conversations.

It is worth noting that when it comes to body language and nonverbal cues, you will be inclined to mirror the body language of your interviewer. Mirroring is when you adapt your body language to those who you are interacting with. An example of this is if your interviewer sits up straight or leans forward you will often feel obliged to do likewise. Understand that this behavior is natural, and you can use it to your advantage. Be as instinctive as possible and avoid being too self-conscious about your mirroring. A small amount of intent will go a long way, and you should not look to copy every movement made by your interviewer.

Let natural conversations flow and stay focused on the content of these discussions, choosing to mirror occasional and relevant gestures to further your connection.

67%
Fail to make
eye contact

38%
Don't smile

Be aware of your nonverbal ques and use them to your advantage to create strong connections with your interviewers.

The interview – conversation flow

Actively listening is one of the most important skills you can bring to an interview. Note that the more an interviewer speaks during your interactions, the more opportunities you'll have to pick up on points and context that you can refer to later in the conversation and when answering questions. Some of these points may be subtle and unintentional. Being present in the moment and mindful of what the interviewer is saying is an essential part of actively listening. You have prepared for various questions and rehearsed how you plan to present your experience and key projects worked on; now is not the time to switch off. Trust in your internal and external preparation. You won't forget your speaking points or answers, but you will lose out on key information if you choose to focus on anything other than your interviewer and the content they are sharing as part of the interview process.

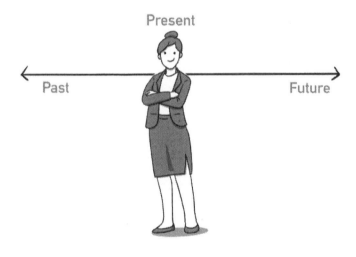

Being present is key to actively listening and being positively engaged in your interview.

The most enjoyable conversations from an interviewer's perspective are those that involve real human connection. While it is important to be professional, humanizing yourself by personalizing your responses and conversations enables them to picture working alongside you. You can achieve this by repeating back key points which have been shared by the interviewer in your own words, prior to articulating your overall thoughts or answering the specific question asked. This method is known as summarizing; it highlights that you are actively engaged in the conversation, and allows for more in-depth discussions and a greater connection with your interviewer. An example of summarizing would be, "It sounds like this company really values collaborating and working in cross functional teams at a high level. Some of the best projects I managed during my time at X company involved working closely with team members across different divisions…"

Summarizing helps you engage with the flow of conversation as well as embrace key topics for further discussion as they come up, through adding your own insight to the discussion. Couple this style with the STAR methodology which we covered earlier and you have a holistic approach and framework to effectively engage with your interviewer.

It is important during your interview to trust in your preparation and to naturally align the content you practiced with the real-time conversations you are having. Remember – your research and preparation gives you a toolkit, not a script. Don't rush to share speaking points you have rehearsed without understanding the context of the question you are being asked. If you do not understand a question, seek clarification before you answer. There's nothing wrong with asking for clarification; it makes your responses seem more calculated and thoughtful. Sharing pre-prepared content that's not actually relevant to the line of questioning reflects negatively on you, and you want to avoid this at all costs. When answering behavioral /situational interview questions about your experience and skills let your preparation shine through by taking the time to phrase your responses and ensure that they are focused and relevant to the question. Above all, relax, actively listen to the questions, take your time in your responses and trust in your preparation.

During the interview, feel confident enough to ask your own questions as well. Saving pre-prepared questions and content for the end of the interview, which many people do, may not be the best strategy. Of course, it's vital that any questions you ask are on topic. Asking questions which are specific to the interviewer and reflect your research will be positively received. One strategy that you can employ in your questioning, if appropriate, is utilizing hypothetical questions to create a sense of already being in the role and working together with your interviewer. This subconscious thinking can further strengthen your relationship with the interviewer and strengthen the overall impression you leave when compared to other candidates. An example of effective hypothetical questioning might be, "Thank you for giving me some insight into the overall organizations strategy for the next six months. I note from my research that the organization has acquired three other companies in the last year to build out its marketing and design capabilities. Should I be successful in joining the team, how would my role support you and the organizations focus on continued growth and further acquisitions?" This example uses effective summarizing that links the content being discussed, in this case, company strategy and growth, with your own possible role in the organization.

Utilizing hypothetical questions connects you with the interviewer at a heightened level by bringing you together around a shared value.

It is worth reiterating your strong interest in the role towards the end of your conversation with each interviewer. Provided you have maintained effective body language throughout your interactions by smiling regularly, maintaining eye contact, and keeping a positive demeanor, these statements will feel genuine and further highlight your overall enthusiasm. You can underscore this by stating your appreciation of the insights shared by the interviewer. Mention that you remain extremely excited at the potential opportunity to work together and that you feel your experience, skills, knowledge, and insights align well with the needs of the role. Weave into your narrative themes from "your story" as discussed earlier in this chapter. If you referenced a desire to grow and further your skills, highlight this by saying something to the effect of, "I see this as an amazing opportunity to join a high performing team where I can apply my skills at a high level while furthering my career development." Afterwards, it may be appropriate to ask what the next steps are in the interview process. Note that if you are meeting with multiple interviewers this is a question that would be best posed to your recruiting contact. When closing an interview, remember to genuinely thank your interviewer for their time and insights.

Interviewing remotely

The COVID-19 pandemic has impacted each and every industry and job market differently. While the process of reviewing and hiring talent has remained the same, the interview experience has shifted significantly towards using more technology-based alternatives. Many candidates during these times have gone through fully remote hiring processes where they have been screened and interviewed without ever meeting a recruiter, hiring manager or interviewer in person. Video conferences have substituted for in-person interviews. This practice is likely to remain common, as many organizations move towards optimizing for remote work; they've realized that great people can be sourced across the country and even internationally. Should your final interview(s) or "in-person" interviews be scheduled as remote web conference interviews, you should still prepare as if you were going to meet in person. Review the video conference notes from chapter 5 to ensure an appropriate and professional set up. Note that the final stages of the interviewing process is still an assessment of how well you can articulate your skills, experience, and knowledge against the role you are interviewing for as well as the strength of your connection with those interviewing you. Whatever the format of the final interview, if you outwork other candidates in these areas and trust in your internal and external preparation to date, you will land the role you thoroughly deserve.

Enjoy your interview no matter what medium is used. Video conferences give you the benefit of being in a comfortable and familiar environment. Trust your investment in yourself and your preparation and you will perform at your best.

Post Interview

Visualization

As you leave the interview room (or log off from the virtual remote interview), take some time to internally picture yourself closing with those who you met with. Mentally rehearse the vision of yourself reporting to your new role, collaborating with team members, and doing some of your best work. Creating positive energy and commitment through visualization manifests particular outcomes in line with the powerful law of attraction theory. By strengthening your connectedness to the workplace, you enhance your odds of attracting a job offer.

Thank you note

Think of your thank you email or note as an additional opportunity to subtly make a case for hiring you, by emphasizing your personal connection with the interviewer(s) and highlighting the best parts of your interactions through the interview process. You can do this by referencing points in your discussions while grounding yourself in gratitude. Be specific and concise; keep it to no more than a few paragraphs. In terms of content and structure, your note should cover the following areas:

1. Opening – thank interviewers – show appreciation for the time taken to discuss the role and organization
2. Highlight an interesting aspect learned from discussions – cover off points which added to your overall understanding
3. Go over a quality or trait that was brought up which you identify with and which further drives your eagerness to work there – this can be a link to strategy, workflow or specific tasks related to the role which came up in your discussion
4. Draw a link to an achievement you would support in this role if successful – tie your skills and experience into a team goal or desired outcome
5. Reiterate your enthusiasm – express eagerness at the potential opportunity to join the organization and work collectively towards positive outcomes
6. Close – professional sign off

Send your thank you note a few hours after your interview. You can use LinkedIn to directly message each interviewer, or alternatively if you have their email address this would be most appropriate means of communication. If you've met with multiple interviewers during your interview process, a best practice would be to send your thank you note to your primary contact. This would likely be the recruiter or hiring manager. They, in turn, will share your message with those who you interviewed with. As part of sending your thank you note to them, checking in regarding next steps would be appropriate at this time, to understand if there are further rounds of interviewing required or when you can expect to hear back from the organization.

A thank you note is a professional courtesy, remember you have already made a great impression in your interview. Aim to keep your note specific and concise.

Personal review

It is likely that you have applied for various other roles during the time you have been engaged in the interview process for this specific job. Reflect on how you feel about the organization. In line with the motivation points made in chapter 1, do you still feel 10 out of 10 in relation to your connectedness to role?

Resignations are often triggered by interpersonal issues and poor work relationships. It is important that you think through your interactions with those who interviewed you, since you will be working closely with them. In particular, do you see yourself getting along with your direct manager? Do you feel that they will provide you with a working environment that will nurture and further your growth and development? Will the team support you and invest in your success? Do you relate to the corporate culture and organizational values? These are the types of questions you should work through following your interview.

You have invested countless hours in your preparation, not just to interview successfully but to take that next step in your career. Use this time to ensure you don't have any doubts should you need to make a decision between accepting this job or another.

Waiting

You have done all you can throughout the interview process to represent yourself in the best possible light. The hardest part is often waiting to hear whether you have been successful. While you might feel a very strong connection to this role and feel as though you did great in the interview, there is unfortunately no guarantee that they'll lead to a formal job offer. Consequently, don't neglect the other roles you have applied for and your preparation for those interviews.

As the chapter closes on interviewing for this specific job, take time to show appreciation for those near and dear to you. The process that you have undertaken in terms of your internal and external preparation has likely taken you away from family and friends in some capacity or limited your time together. Avoid letting your mind wander to the outcome of your interview; be present with those close to you, practicing thankfulness for their support during this period.

Even if the recruiting manager has not explicitly said so, be aware that there may be a need to interview yet another time in a second final-round interview. If this is communicated to you, view this as highly positive and reflective of the fact that through the interview process you have made a good impression and they think you're a good fit for the role. Subsequent in-person interviews or second-round interviews are sometimes required to sign off on a hiring decision; you may be meeting with executives or "higher-ups" who have an interest in the role given its interactions with their teams or strategy. If you are called back for a second final-round interview, remain persistent in your preparation and approach; know who is interviewing you, stay abreast of organizational news, and focus on making connections and articulating your strengths. Remember, you have been through the process once already. Remain confident in your abilities to connect and present yourself well, and you will be successful.

Interviewing is a journey, filled with various elements of self-discovery and learning. Even after you land your dream job of today, chances are that, in time, you will interview again as you continue your career trajectory. Unfortunately, you may also find out that despite all of your preparation you did not get the job. Note that this decision is largely outside of your control. As hard as it can be given the time, effort and investment you have made in your internal and external preparation, don't be hard on yourself. See this as progress in your own personal journey and look to learn from the process.

To harness and further understand your learnings from your final interview(s) reflect on how they went and what key takeaways you found. Think through how these interactions were different from the screening process, how you built connections and answered questions, how your non-verbal cues and body language supported your presentation, and how your internal and external preparation set you up for success. Think through what you would approach differently next time. Done correctly, you will feel positive about your overall engagement and have areas that you can build upon when you interview again.

Chapter Summary

Positively interviewing and gaining an offer of employment correlates directly to how you prepare and manage yourself through the final interview phases. From pre-interview planning and factfinding to post-interview initiatives, how you apply yourself in relation to the areas outlined enables you to present the best version of yourself as you interview. Your strategy and preparedness for answering questions must also be supported by your body language, nonverbal cues, and ability to make a strong connection with your interviewers to heighten your success. Noting the level of internal and external preparation you have taken in the lead up to this point and the interactions with the recruiting process to date, keep your preparations for this phase targeted and specific as outlined through this chapter. Finally, trust the totality of your preparation to date as you engage in conversations and you will make a positive impression, setting yourself up for an offer of employment for your dream role.

Conclusion

Successfully navigating any challenge is a matter of motivation and progression. Interviewing is no different. As long as you internalize your motivations and use them to establish and maintain momentum, you will achieve your desired outcome. We've outlined various areas of internal and external preparation to review, reflect, and focus on, setting you up for success in creating and maintaining your own personal momentum for your interview journey. I sincerely hope you find it useful as you chase your dreams in building and furthering your career. Should you wish to discuss any of the content covered within this publication or aspects of your personal interview preparation, the author, Y.P. can be reached at coach.mindfulprep@gmail.com and offers tailored coaching, feedback and guidance.

Now get out there and reach for the stars!

Made in the USA
Monee, IL
26 November 2024

71382812R00063